PAPER CREATIONS: GREAT PAPER AIRPLANES

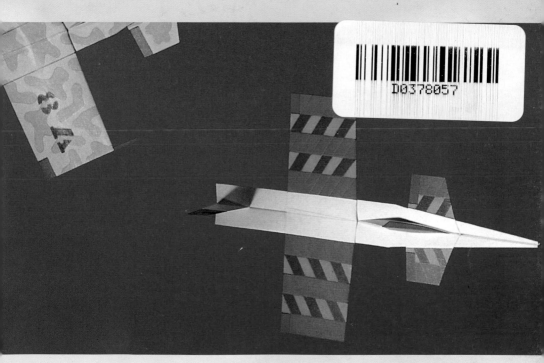

Norman Schmidt

STERLING
INNOVATION
A Division of Sterling Publishing Co., Inc.
New York

10 9 8 7 6 5 4 3 2 1

PUBLISHED BY STERLING PUBLISHING CO., INC.
387 PARK AVENUE SOUTH, NEW YORK, NY 10016

THIS BOOK IS EXCERPTED FROM THE FOLLOWING STERLING/TAMOS TITLES:
BEST EVER PAPER AIRPLANES © 1994 BY NORMAN SCHMIDT
SUPER PAPER AIRPLANES © 1994 BY NORMAN SCHMIDT

DISTRIBUTED IN CANADA BY STERLING PUBLISHING
C/O CANADIAN MANDA GROUP, 165 DUFFERIN STREET
TORONTO, ONTARIO, CANADA M6K 3H6
DISTRIBUTED IN THE UNITED KINGDOM BY GMC DISTRIBUTION SERVICES
CASTLE PLACE, 166 HIGH STREET, LEWES, EAST SUSSEX, ENGLAND BN7 1XU
DISTRIBUTED IN AUSTRALIA BY CAPRICORN LINK (AUSTRALIA) PTY. LTD.
P.O. BOX 704, WINDSOR, NSW 2756, AUSTRALIA

PRINTED IN CHINA

STERLING ISBN-13: 978-1-4027-4943-8
          ISBN-10: 1-4027-4943-0

FOR INFORMATION ABOUT CUSTOM EDITIONS, SPECIAL SALES, PREMIUM
AND CORPORATE PURCHASES, PLEASE CONTACT STERLING SPECIAL SALES
DEPARTMENT AT 800-805-5489 OR SPECIALSALES@STERLINGPUB.COM.

Contents

Flight

People have been obsessed with the idea of flight ever since they looked into the sky and saw birds soaring gently overhead. Mythical stories in many cultures around the world have flying creatures of all sorts, including human beings. When did the reality of human flight begin?

Archeologists in Egypt have discovered a small wooden bird, carved from lightweight sycamore wood, that has a very aerodynamic shape. This small wooden bird is unlike any real bird because its tail has both horizontal and vertical surfaces, just like present-day airplanes. It is not known whether this was a toy, a weather vane, or a small model of some larger craft.

There are other examples of flying toys, such as the Saqqara bird invented by the Greek philosopher Archytas in about 345 B.C. It was a small wooden dove attached to an arm that allowed it to "lift off" in wavering flight. It is not known how the bird was propelled. At about the same time, the Chinese philosopher Mo Tzu constructed what was possibly the first kite, which is simply a tethered airplane. Some Europeans made wings of wood, cloth, and bird feathers, strapped them to their arms, and jumped off high buildings. In 1020, Eilmer "the flying monk" did this, and attained some success with flight, but broke both his legs in the attempt. In the 1500s, the artist and inventor Leonardo da Vinci made many drawings and models of different kinds of aircraft, including the parachute. Another story from the 1700s tells of a French locksmith named Besnier who, with wings strapped to his arms and legs, jumped from a tall building and glided over neighboring houses.

The development of kites continued, and they became the forerunners of free-flying airplanes. European inventors and scientists used them to carry out experiments in aerodynamic forces. Such experiments led to the first free-flying airplanes of Sir George Cayley in the 1790s. They demonstrated the principles of flight as they are understood today. In the 1850s Sir George's coachman was among the first people to fly in an actual airplane. The stage was now set for the development of controllable airplanes.

Construction

When carefully made, the paper airplanes in this book are super flyers. They can be built using the paper included, or ordinary 20 or 24 lb bond copier paper measuring $8^1/_2$ inches by 11 inches (21.6 cm by 27.9 cm). Bond paper is lightweight, easy to cut and fold, and easy to fasten together. It is available in a variety of colors (black paper may have to be purchased at an art store). Since a paper airplane's lift and thrust are limited, every effort must be made to keep drag at a minimum. Every surface not parallel to the direction of travel (wings, nose, and canopy) adds drag, so the neater and more accurate your construction, the better the plane will fly. Clean and accurate cuts and crisp folds are a top priority.

MEASURING AND CUTTING

Use a sharp pencil to mark the measurements and draw firm, accurate lines. Cut out pieces with a sharp pair of scissors or a craft knife and a steel-edged ruler. A knife makes a cleaner cut. When using a knife be sure to work on a proper cutting surface.

FOLDING

Always lay the paper on a level surface for folding. Folding is easier along a score line (an indented line on the paper made with a hard pencil drawn along a ruler). There are only four kinds of folds used in making the airplanes in this book. They are mountain folds, valley folds, sink folds, and reverse folds. Where multiple layers are folded, run your fingers back and forth along the fold, pressing hard to make a sharp crease.

GLUING

A glue stick works well for paper airplanes. Follow the instructions for gluing. Cover the entire contacting surfaces that are to be joined. If there are multiple layers, apply glue to each of the sheets. Glue should be used sparingly, but use enough to hold the parts together. Where multiple layers are being joined, you may need to hold the pieces for a few minutes until the glue sets.

Mountain Fold   **Valley Fold**   **Sink Fold**   **Reverse Fold**

A **MOUNTAIN FOLD** and a **VALLEY FOLD** are actually the same kind of fold. Both are made by folding a flat piece of paper and sharply creasing the fold line. The only difference is that one folds up (valley fold) and the other folds down (mountain fold). They are distinguished only for convenience in giving instructions.

To make a **SINK FOLD**, begin with paper that has been folded using a mountain (or valley) fold and measure as required across the folded corner. Then push in the corner along the measured lines, making a diagonal fold. Finish by creasing the folds sharply.

To make a **REVERSE FOLD**, begin with paper that has been folded using a mountain (or valley) fold and measure as required, down from the top and in from the edge. Then cut along line from the top (heavy line). Push cut piece in, as shown. Finish by creasing folds sharply.

Trimming for Flight

Air is made up of small, solid, evenly spaced particles called molecules. Everything in the universe is made up of molecules, but air molecules are quite far apart compared with those that make up metal, wood, or paper, and they are easily separated when a body moves through them. The molecules are piled up in a thick layer from the ground, and this is called the atmosphere. It forms part of the space around us and the sky above us. This layer of air molecules (atmosphere) exerts pressure on everything in the world, and it is this pressure that makes flight possible. The shape of the airplane affects the molecules as they move across the airplane's surfaces, increasing or decreasing air pressure, determining the flight characteristics of the plane.

No paper airplanes are perfectly straight. And they are easily bent. Shown on page 8 is an example of trimming using the rudder. Airplane A flies straight

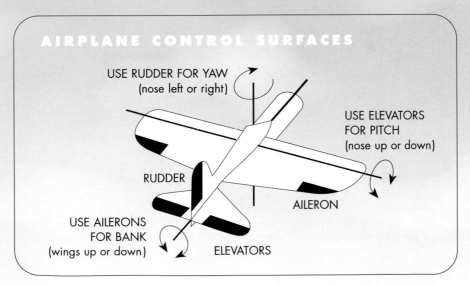

AIRPLANE CONTROL SURFACES

USE RUDDER FOR YAW
(nose left or right)

USE ELEVATORS
FOR PITCH
(nose up or down)

RUDDER

AILERON

USE AILERONS
FOR BANK
(wings up or down)

ELEVATORS

because air flows smoothly along its surfaces. It needs no trim. Airplane B yaws to its left because the air on the left is deflected by the bent fuselage, increasing air pressure on that side. The rudder is used to compensate. Airplane C again flies straight because it has been trimmed so that the deflected air on the left is opposed by air being deflected by the rudder on the right. But airplane C does not fly as well as airplane A because it is creating much more drag.

Before making any trim adjustments to a paper airplane that you have just constructed, be sure you are releasing the plane correctly for flight. Always begin with a gentle straight-ahead release, keeping the wings level. Hold the plane between thumb and forefinger just behind the center of gravity. As your technique improves, you can throw harder, adjusting the trim as needed. But remember, all planes do not fly at the same speed.

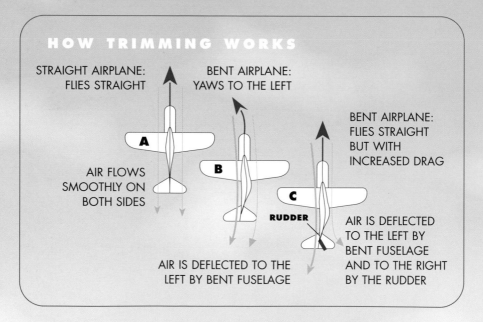

HOW TRIMMING WORKS

STRAIGHT AIRPLANE:
FLIES STRAIGHT

BENT AIRPLANE:
YAWS TO THE LEFT

BENT AIRPLANE:
FLIES STRAIGHT
BUT WITH
INCREASED DRAG

A

AIR FLOWS
SMOOTHLY ON
BOTH SIDES

B

C

RUDDER

AIR IS DEFLECTED TO THE
LEFT BY BENT FUSELAGE

AIR IS DEFLECTED
TO THE LEFT BY
BENT FUSELAGE
AND TO THE RIGHT
BY THE RUDDER

NOTE: Fly Safely. Some of the airplanes in this book have sharp points, so never fly them towards another person. If you fly the airplanes outdoors they may go farther than you expect. Be sure they do not go into the street where you will have to retrieve them.

Flying Tips

Don't be discouraged if on first flight your paper airplane "corkscrews" and crashes. Flying paper airplanes is a delicate balancing act. Only when everything works in harmony—wings, horizontal tail, vertical tail, and control surfaces—is successful flight achieved. With each paper airplane that you build, aim to improve the construction. When carefully made and trimmed, the paper airplanes in this book are super flyers. But remember, the performance of each airplane differs. Experimentation is necessary in order to achieve maximum performance. This is part of the fun of flying paper planes.

Folds that are not neat and crisp add drag to the airplane. This will decrease glide performance. Sloppy folds can also result in twisted airplanes. Inaccurate gluing does not help matters. A twisted plane is sure to "corkscrew" badly (see below). The importance of careful folds cannot be overemphasized.

Airplanes must be symmetrical—one side must be just like the other. On both sides wing and horizontal tail sizes, shapes, and thicknesses must be the same. Also make sure that the control surfaces on one side are the same sizes and are bent the same amount as on the other side.

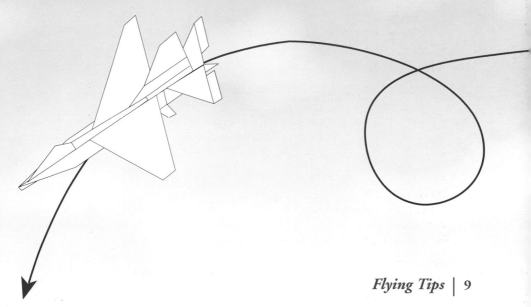

Make sure that the dihedral (upward slanting of wings and tail) is adjusted correctly. In each design, refer to the last step of construction for suggestions. Sometimes experimentation with a different dihedral (or none at all) will be successful. Dihedral provides stability; however, too much dihedral has a destabilizing effect.

Some of the airplanes in this book have secondary control surfaces (flaps). Secondary control surfaces need special attention. If they are bent down slightly, lift is increased. If they are bent down 90°, drag is greatly increased and the nose will pitch down. Additional up elevator is needed, increasing the angle of attack but also increasing drag. Trimmed in this way an airplane does not glide very far. In full-sized airplanes, this trim is good for landing. Experiment with different settings of the secondary control surfaces. Adjust carefully for best results.

Paper airplanes are not baseballs. They cannot be thrown hard. To launch, hold the fuselage lightly between thumb and forefinger near the point where the plane balances. Throw with a firm forward motion, keeping the nose level, pushing the airplane more than throwing it. With a bit of practice you will discover just how hard each of the planes need to be thrown under different conditions.

PITCH TRIM

Although the paper airplanes in this book are built to resemble a bird or powered aircraft, they are obviously all gliders. For thrust they must convert altitude into airspeed. The pitching axis is very important in determining airspeed. Once properly trimmed, an airplane will always fly at the same speed. If the airplane zooms toward the ground, bend the elevators up slightly to raise the nose.

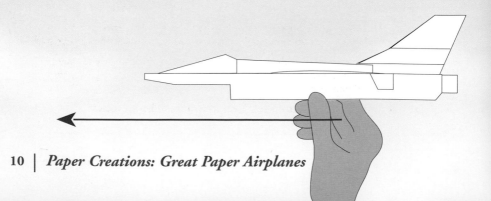

If more speed is needed, as in an outdoor flight, less up elevator will produce the desired result.

ROLL TRIM

Providing the wings are not twisted, the wings should remain more or less level in flight. If one wing drops, bend the aileron down slightly on that wing and up slightly on the other wing.

YAW TRIM

If the plane still has a tendency to turn, bend the rudder slightly opposite to the direction of the turn.

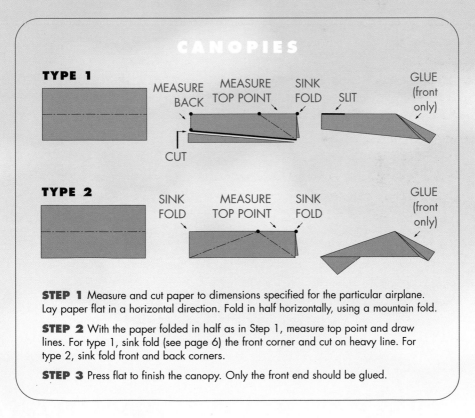

CANOPIES

TYPE 1
MEASURE BACK MEASURE TOP POINT SINK FOLD SLIT GLUE (front only)
CUT

TYPE 2
SINK FOLD MEASURE TOP POINT SINK FOLD GLUE (front only)

STEP 1 Measure and cut paper to dimensions specified for the particular airplane. Lay paper flat in a horizontal direction. Fold in half horizontally, using a mountain fold.

STEP 2 With the paper folded in half as in Step 1, measure top point and draw lines. For type 1, sink fold (see page 6) the front corner and cut on heavy line. For type 2, sink fold front and back corners.

STEP 3 Press flat to finish the canopy. Only the front end should be glued.

Coot

BACKGROUND INFORMATION

This airplane is called the "Coot" because it is designed with a heavy body. It resembles the stubby body and short wings of the duck-like bird of the same name. This airplane is a modified delta (triangle) wing design. It is shaped like some of today's fighter planes, such as the Grumman F14, when it is in high-speed trim.

TECHNICAL INFORMATION

The Coot is designed with a canopy for added realism. Make sure that its shape is properly adjusted, with no dihedral (upward slanting of wings) when in flight. Hold it between thumb and forefinger, launching it briskly straight ahead.

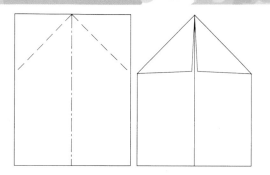

STEP 1 Lay the paper flat in a vertical direction. Fold paper in half vertically, using a mountain fold. Unfold. Then valley fold upper corners to the center crease.

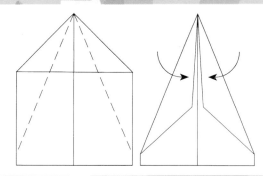

STEP 2 Valley fold upper diagonals along broken lines to meet center crease.

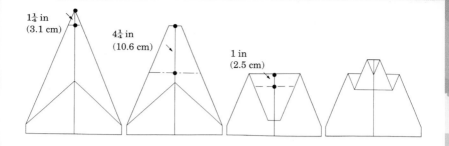

STEP 3 Measure down from tip along center crease, as shown, and make a mountain fold. Measure from fold along center crease, as shown, and mountain fold again. Flip airplane over. From fold, measure down along center crease and valley fold, as shown.

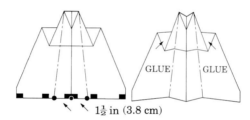

STEP 4 Measure as indicated from center crease and mountain fold to top corners to form fuselage and wings. Unfold. Make control surfaces. On each side, glue where shown.

AILERONS, ELEVATORS, & RUDDER ½ in x ¼ in (1.3 cm x .6 cm)

NOTE: In the instructions, control surfaces (elevators, ailerons, rudder) are shown in black. The cuts are always ¼ inch deep on ends only, but widths vary. Their dimensions are always written as follows:

1 IN x ¼ IN (2.5 CM x .6 CM) OR
½ IN x ¼ IN (1.3 CM x .6 CM)

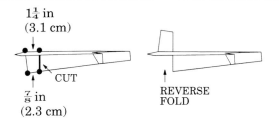

$1\frac{1}{4}$ in
(3.1 cm)

CUT

$\frac{7}{8}$ in
(2.3 cm)

REVERSE
FOLD

STEP 5 Measure and mark as indicated along back of fuselage and cut along heavy line. Then reverse fold to finish vertical tail (see page 6).

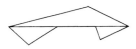

STEP 6 Make the type 2 canopy (see page 11).

CANOPY (type 2) 2 in x 5 ½ (5 cm x 14 cm) with top point 1 ½ in (3.8 cm) from front tip

GLUE
(nose only)

STEP 7 Insert canopy into fuselage to align with nose. Glue in place, applying glue only to the inside nose area of fuselage and the small triangle of the canopy. Leave the back to flare open. Wings should have no dihedral.

Thrush

BACKGROUND INFORMATION

This airplane is called the "Thrush" because of its slender shape and pointed nose that resembles the slim body and long beak of the bird. It is a modified delta wing design (triangle). Its twin vertical tails are amid-ship, like those on the McDonnell Douglas F18.

TECHNICAL INFORMATION

Hold the Trush between thumb and forefinger, launching it straight ahead. This paper airplane performs well indoors and out, even in brisk wind.

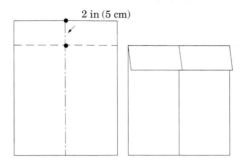

2 in (5 cm)

STEP 1 Lay paper flat in a vertical direction. Fold paper in half vertically using a mountain fold. Unfold. Then measure down from top along center fold and draw a line. Valley fold on this line.

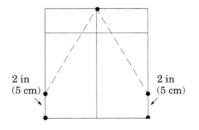

2 in (5 cm)   2 in (5 cm)

STEP 2 Measure and draw lines as shown. Valley fold along these lines. Unfold.

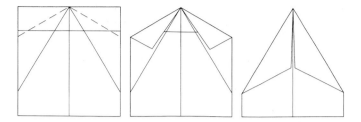

STEP 3 On each side, valley fold so that upper edge meets diagonal crease. Refold original diagonal creases.

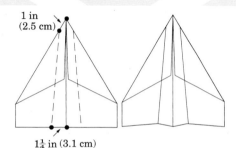

1 in
(2.5 cm)

1¼ in (3.1 cm)

STEP 4 On each side of center crease, measure and draw lines as indicated. Valley fold along these lines. Unfold.

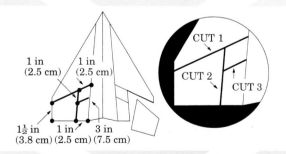

CUT 1

CUT 2

CUT 3

1 in
(2.5 cm)

1 in
(2.5 cm)

1½ in   1 in   3 in
(3.8 cm) (2.5 cm) (7.5 cm)

STEP 5 Flip airplane over. On each side, measure and draw lines, as shown. Cut along these lines (see inset), and discard paper.

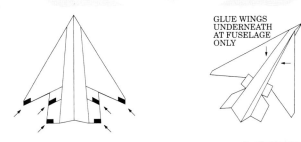

STEP 6 Glue nose only, and let back flare open. Adjust so that, when viewed from back, it makes a shape as indicated.

AILERONS, ELEVATORS, & RUDDER ½ in x ¼ in (1.3 cm x .6 cm)

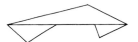

STEP 7 Make a type 2 canopy. (See page 11.)

CANOPY (type 2) 1 in X 3 in (2.5 cm x 7.5 cm) with top point 1 in (2.5 cm) from front tip

GLUE
NOSE
ONLY

VIEW FROM BACK

STEP 8 Insert canopy into fuselage so that front diagonal edges align. Apply glue only to small triangle of the canopy and the front of the fuselage, allowing the back to flare open. Adjust the wings to have no dihedral (upward slanting). The vertical tails should be almost vertical, and the horizontal tail should have anhedral (downward slanting).

Merganser

BACKGROUND INFORMATION

This airplane is called the "Merganser" because of its slender fuselage which resembles the slender body of the bird. This paper airplane is modeled on fighter planes of conventional design with straight tapered wings, such as the Canadair CL114 Tutor, the Lockheed T33, and the Lockheed F104.

TECHNICAL INFORMATION

When carefully made, this airplane will go fast and far. It is maneuverable and can be trimmed for flying straight or for aerobatics, both indoors and out. Launch by holding between thumb and forefinger.

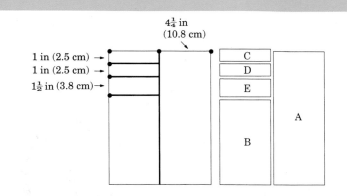

STEP 1 Measure and cut the various pieces from a sheet of bond paper.

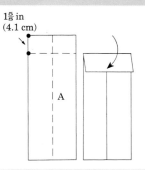

STEP 2 To make the fuselage, fold piece A in half vertically using a valley fold. Unfold. Measure from top and valley fold, as shown.

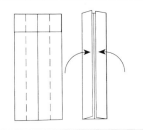 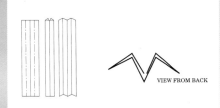

STEP 3 Valley fold each side so that outer edges meet center crease, as shown.

STEP 4 Fold each side again using a mountain fold, so that outer edges meet center crease at back. Then adjust folds so that paper looks like an upside-down W, as shown.

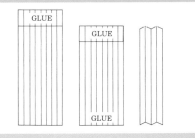 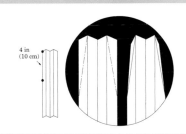

STEP 5 Unfold fuselage completely. Refold applying glue to contacting surfaces, as shown. Make sure fuselage is straight.

STEP 6 On each side, measure from top (front of fuselage), mark, and mountain fold, as shown in enlarged view.

STEP 7 Flip over fuselage. On each side, valley fold triangle along broken lines, matching fold line to existing crease.

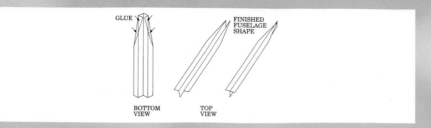

STEP 8 Glue triangles. Hold in place until glue sets. It is important that the fuselage stays straight. Do not glue nose yet.

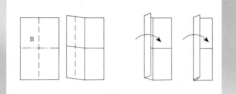

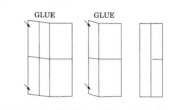

STEP 9 Use piece B to make the wings. Fold in half vertically, using a valley fold. Unfold. Fold in half horizontally using a mountain fold. Unfold. Then valley fold left side vertically so that one outer edge meets center crease. Fold over again along original vertical center crease.

STEP 10 Unfold completely. Refold, applying glue to no more than 1 in (2.5 cm) from outer tips, as shown. The folded over part is the bottom of the leading edge (front) of the wings.

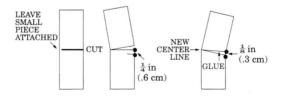

STEP 11 To taper wings, cut along center line from the trailing edge (back), leaving a small piece attached at the leading edge. Then measure and make a mark on trailing edge, as shown. Align pieces to the mark. Glue. Measure and draw a new center line.

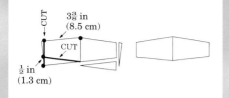

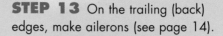

STEP 12 To finish tapered wings, measure, draw, and cut wingtips and trailing edges along heavy lines, as indicated.

STEP 13 On the trailing (back) edges, make ailerons (see page 14).

AILERONS ¹/₂ in x ¹/₄ in (1.2 cm x .6 cm)

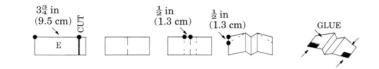

STEP 14 Use piece E to make the horizontal tail. Cut to dimensions indicated. Valley fold in half vertically. Unfold. On each side, measure from center crease, as shown, and mountain fold. On each side, measure and mountain fold leading edge along broken lines. Glue. Make elevators on trailing edges (see page 14).

ELEVATORS ³/₄ in x ¹/₄ in (1.9 cm x .6 cm)

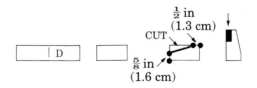

STEP 15 Use piece D to make the vertical tail. Valley fold in half vertically and glue together. Then measure and cut along heavy line, as shown. Make rudder on trailing edge (see page 14).

RUDDER ³/₄ in x ¹/₄ in (1.9 cm x .6 cm)

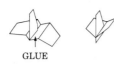

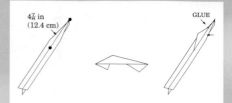

STEP 16 Join pieces D and E to finish tail. Apply glue and slide D into center of E, aligning trailing edges.

STEP 17 Use piece C to make a type 2 canopy (see page 11). Measure from front of fuselage and mark. Use this dot for positioning back of canopy. Apply glue to inside of nose and the small triangles on the bottom of canopy. Hold until glue sets.

CANOPY (type 2) 1 in x 3 in (2.5 cm x 7.5 cm) with top point 2 in (5 cm) from front tip

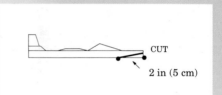

STEP 18 Use dot (back of canopy) for positioning leading edge of wings. Glue in place, making sure wings are centered and at right angles to the fuselage. Apply glue and slide tail into back of fuselage so that trailing edges align.

STEP 19 Measure and cut front of fuselage diagonally along heavy line to finish nose.

BACK VIEW

STEP 20 Adjust dihedral (upward slanting) of wings and horizontal tail, as shown.

Duck

BACKGROUND INFORMATION

This paper airplane is called the "Duck" because of its long slim shape. It is modeled on the airplane known as a "canard" which is French for duck. Canard airplanes have the wings positioned toward the back of the fuselage and the horizontal "tail" — known as canard wings — toward the front. The Beech Starship and the Saab 37 Viggen are examples of such a design.

TECHNICAL INFORMATION

When carefully made, this airplane is very stable in the air and has a flat glide. It will go fast and far. It can be trimmed to fly straight or it can be made to do aerobatics. Launch the plane by holding it between thumb and forefinger. Notice that in order to trim for nose up, the elevators must be bent down.

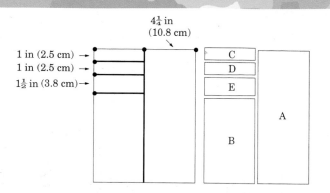

STEP 1 Measure and cut the various pieces from a sheet of bond paper.

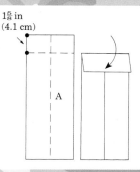

STEP 2 To make the fuselage, fold piece A in half vertically using a valley fold. Unfold. Measure from top and valley fold, as shown.

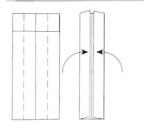

VIEW FROM BACK

STEP 3 Valley fold each side so that outer edges meet the center crease, as shown.

STEP 4 Fold each side again using a mountain fold, so that outer edges meet center crease at back. Then adjust folds so that paper looks like an upside-down W, as shown.

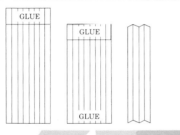

GLUE

GLUE

GLUE

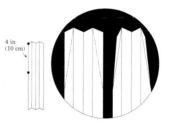

4 in
(10 cm)

STEP 5 Unfold fuselage completely. Refold applying glue to contacting surfaces, as shown. Make sure fuselage is straight.

STEP 6 On each side, measure from top (front of fuselage), mark, and mountain fold along broken lines, as shown in enlarged view.

STEP 7 Flip over fuselage. On each side, valley fold triangle along broken lines, matching fold line to existing crease.

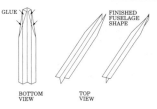

STEP 8 Glue triangles. Hold in place until glue sets. It is important that the fuselage stays straight. Do not glue nose yet.

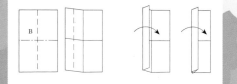

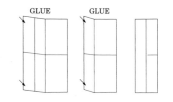

STEP 9 Use piece B to make the wings. Fold in half vertically, using a valley fold. Unfold. Fold in half horizontally using a mountain fold. Unfold. Then valley fold vertically so that one outer edge meets center crease. Fold over again along original vertical center crease.

STEP 10 Unfold completely. Refold, applying glue to no more than 1 in (2.5 cm) from outer tips, as shown. The folded over part is the bottom of the leading edge (front) of the wings.

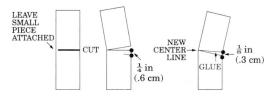

STEP 11 To taper wings, cut along center heavy line from the trailing (back) edge, leaving a small piece attached at the leading (front) edge. Then measure and make a mark on trailing edge, as shown. Align pieces to the mark. Glue. Measure and draw a new center line.

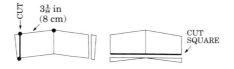

STEP 12 To finish tapered wings, measure and cut wing tips along heavy lines. Then, using a ruler to mark, cut trailing edge square, as shown.

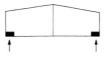

STEP 13 On the trailing edges, make ailerons (see page 14).

AILERONS ¹/₂ in x ¹/₄ in (1.3 cm x .6 cm)

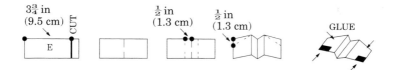

STEP 14 Use piece E to make the canard wing. Cut to dimensions indicated. Valley fold in half vertically. Unfold. On each side, measure from center crease, as shown, and mountain fold. On each side, measure and mountain fold leading edge along broken lines. Glue. Make elevators on trailing edges (see page 14).

ELEVATORS ³/₄ in x ¹/₄ in (1.9 cm x .6 cm)

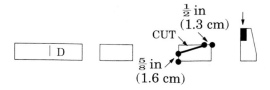

STEP 15 Use piece D to make the vertical tail. Valley fold in half vertically and glue together. Then measure and cut along heavy line, as shown. Make rudder on trailing edge (see page 14).

RUDDER ¾ in x ¼ in (1.9 cm x .6 cm).

STEP 16 Measure from front of fuselage, as shown, and make mark A for positioning leading edge of canard wings and front of canopy, and mark B for positioning leading edge of main wings.

STEP 17 Use piece C to make a type 2 canopy (see page 11). Apply glue to inside of nose, the bottom of the canard wings, and the small triangles on the bottom of canopy. Slide in place together and hold until glue sets.

**CANOPY (type 2) 1 in X 3 in (2.5 cm x 7.5 cm)
with top point 2 in (5 cm) from front tip**

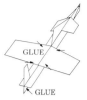

STEP 18 Glue main wings in place, with leading edge at mark B, making sure wings are centered and at right angles to the fuselage. Apply glue and slide vertical tail into back of fuselage so that trailing edges align.

CUT
2 in (5 cm)

STEP 19 Measure and cut front of fuselage diagonally along heavy line to finish nose.

BACK VIEW

STEP 20 Adjust dihedral (upward slanting) of main wings and anhedral (downward slanting) of canard wings, as shown.

Grebe

BACKGROUND INFORMATION

This paper airplane is called the "Grebe" because of its similarity to the duck-like grebe which has a very short tail and stubby wings. This paper airplane is a delta (triangle) wing airplane. It has no horizontal tail. It is modeled on delta wing fighter planes such as the General Dynamics F106 and the Dassault-Breguet Mirage 2000.

TECHNICAL INFORMATION

This airplane can be made to go fast and far. It can be trimmed to fly straight or it can be made to do aerobatics. But it is sensitive to pitch trim. Launch the plane by holding it between thumb and forefinger.

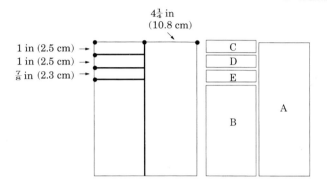

STEP 1 Measure and cut the various pieces from a sheet of bond paper.

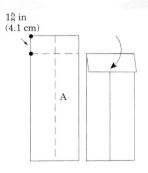

STEP 2 To make the fuselage, fold piece A in half vertically using a valley fold. Unfold. Measure from top and valley fold, as shown.

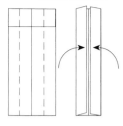 

STEP 3 Valley fold each side so that outer edges meet center crease, as shown.

STEP 4 Fold each side again using a mountain fold, so that outer edges meet center crease at back. Then adjust folds so that paper looks like an upside-down W, as shown.

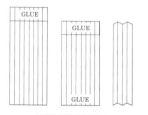 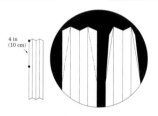

STEP 5 Unfold fuselage completely. Refold applying glue to contacting surfaces, as shown. Make sure fuselage is straight.

STEP 6 On each side, measure from top (front of fuselage), mark, and mountain fold along broken lines, as shown in enlarged view.

STEP 7 Flip over fuselage. On each side, valley fold triangle along broken lines, matching fold line to existing crease.

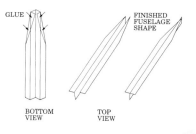

GLUE

FINISHED
FUSELAGE
SHAPE

BOTTOM
VIEW

TOP
VIEW

STEP 8 Glue triangles. Hold in place until glue sets. It is important that the fuselage stays straight. Do not glue nose yet.

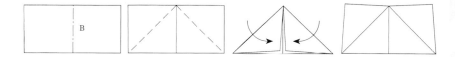

B

STEP 9 Use piece B to make the wings. Fold in half horizontally using a mountain fold. Unfold. On each side, valley fold diagonally so that upper edge meets center crease. Unfold.

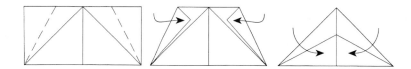

STEP 10 On each side, valley fold diagonally, so that outer edge meets previously made diagonal crease. Fold over again along the original diagonal creases.

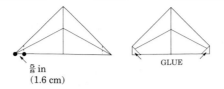

$\frac{5}{8}$ in
(1.6 cm)

GLUE

STEP 11 On each side, measure in from the wingtip and draw a line, indicated by broken line. Valley fold along this line. Glue the small triangle.

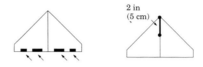

2 in
(5 cm)

STEP 12 Flip wings over. On each side, in from the wingtip at the point of the triangles, make aileron on trailing (back) edge (see page 14). Make elevator adjacent to the aileron. Then cut a slit along center crease, as shown by heavy line.

ELEVATORS 1 in x ¹/₄ in (2.5 cm x .6 cm)
AILERONS ¹/₂ in x ¹/₄ in (1.3 cm x .6 cm)

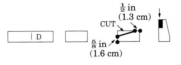

$\frac{1}{2}$ in
(1.3 cm)

CUT

D

$\frac{5}{8}$ in
(1.6 cm)

STEP 13 Use piece D to make the vertical tail. Valley fold in half vertically and glue together. Then measure and cut, as indicated by heavy line. Make rudder on trailing edge (see page 14).

RUDDER ³/₄ in x ¹/₄ in (1.9 cm x .6 cm)

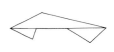
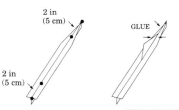

STEP 14 Use piece C to make a type 2 canopy (see page 11). Measure from front of fuselage, as shown, and make a mark for positioning the front of canopy. Measure from back of fuselage and make a mark for positioning the trailing edge of the wings. Apply glue to inside of nose and the small triangles on the bottom of canopy. Slide canopy in place and hold until glue sets.

**CANOPY (type 2) 1 in X 3 in (2.5 cm x 7.5 cm)
with top point 2 in (5 cm) from front tip**

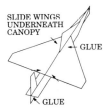

STEP 15 Apply glue to wings and slide them underneath the canopy. Align trailing edge to the mark. Make sure wings are centered and at right angles to the fuselage. Then apply glue and slide vertical tail into back of fuselage so that trailing edges align.

STEP 16 Measure and cut front of fuselage diagonally along heavy line to finish nose.

STEP 17 This airplane has no dihedral (upward slanting) or anhedral (downward slanting) of wings.

Tern

BACKGROUND INFORMATION

This paper airplane is called the "Tern" because its wings are turned forward, instead of being swept back, as is common. While the bird's wings are not swept forward, they are sharply bent. This paper airplane is modeled on the Grumman X29 experimental airplane, an airplane that is controlled by on-board computers. In addition to having unusual wings, it is also a canard design.

TECHNICAL INFORMATION

This unusual airplane will fly fast and it is very maneuverable. Its construction is similar to the preceding three airplanes. This airplane is sensitive to pitch trim. Launch the plane by holding it firmly between thumb and forefinger.

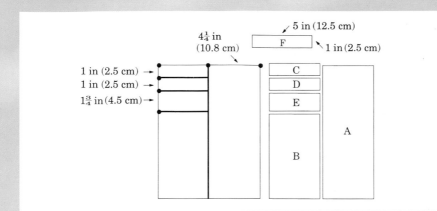

STEP 1 Measure and cut the various pieces from a sheet of bond paper. One additional piece is needed, as shown.

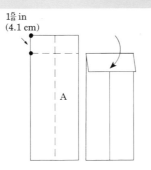

STEP 2 To make the fuselage, fold piece A in half vertically using a valley fold. Unfold. Measure from top and valley fold, as shown.

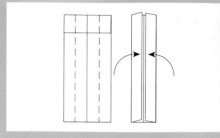
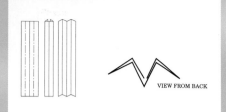

STEP 3 Valley fold each side so that outer edges meet center crease, as shown.

STEP 4 Fold each side again using a mountain fold, so that outer edges meet center crease at back. Then adjust folds so that paper looks like an upside-down W, as shown.

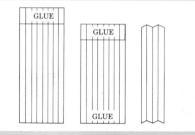
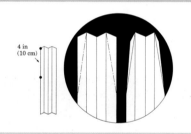

STEP 5 Unfold fuselage completely. Refold applying glue to contacting surfaces, as shown. Make sure fuselage is straight.

STEP 6 On each side, measure from top (front of fuselage), mark, and mountain fold along broken lines, as shown in enlarged view.

STEP 7 Flip over fuselage. On each side, valley fold triangle along broken lines, matching fold line to existing crease.

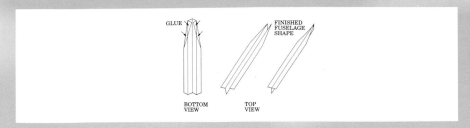

STEP 8 Glue triangles. Hold in place until glue sets. It is important that the fuselage stays straight. Do not glue nose yet.

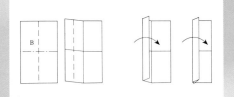 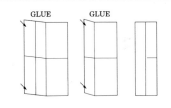

STEP 9 Use piece B to make the wings. Fold in half vertically, using a valley fold. Unfold. Fold in half horizontally using a mountain fold. Unfold. Then valley fold vertically so that one outer edge meets center crease. Fold over again along original vertical center crease.

STEP 10 Unfold completely. Refold, applying glue to no more than 1 in (2.5 cm) from outer tips, as shown. The folded over part is the bottom of the leading edge (front) of the wings.

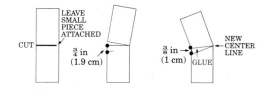

STEP 11 To sweep wings forward, cut along center line from the leading (front) edge, leaving a small piece attached at the trailing (back) edge. Then measure and make a mark on leading edge, as shown. Align pieces to the mark. Glue. Measure and draw a new center line.

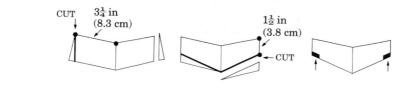

STEP 12 To finish forward swept wings, measure and cut wing tips along heavy lines. Then cut trailing edge along heavy lines, as shown. On trailing edges, make ailerons (see page 14).

AILERONS ¹/₂ in x ¹/₄ in (1.3 cm x .6 cm)

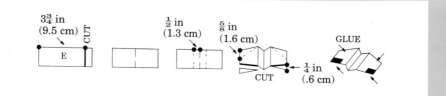

STEP 13 Use piece E to make the canard wing. Cut to dimensions as indicated. Valley fold in half vertically. Unfold. On each side, measure from center crease, as shown, and mountain fold. On each side, measure and mountain fold leading edge along broken lines. Glue. Cut trailing edges and make elevators (see page 14).

ELEVATORS ³/₄ in x ¹/₄ in (1.9 cm x .6 cm)

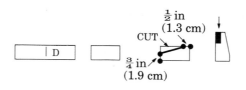

STEP 14 Use piece D to make the vertical tail. Valley fold in half vertically and glue together. Then measure and cut along heavy line, as shown. Make rudder on trailing edge (see page 14).

RUDDER ³/₄ in x ¹/₄ in (1.9 cm x .6 cm)

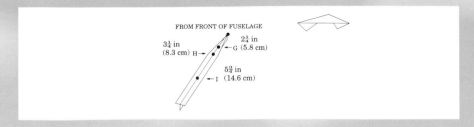

FROM FRONT OF FUSELAGE

3¼ in
(8.3 cm) H

2¼ in
G (5.8 cm)

5¾ in
I (14.6 cm)

STEP 15 Use piece C to make a type 2 canopy (see page 11). Measure from front of fuselage and make marks for positioning the leading edges of canopy at G, canard wings at H, and main wings at I, as shown.

CANOPY (type 2) 1 in X 3 in (2.5 cm x 7.5 cm)
with top point 1¹/₄ in (3.1 cm) from front tip

GLUE

GLUE

GLUE

STEP 16 Apply glue to inside of nose, the bottom of the canard wings, and the small triangles on the bottom of canopy. Slide in place together and hold until glue sets.

STEP 17 Glue main wings in place, making sure they are centered and at right angles to the fuselage. Apply glue and slide vertical tail into back of fuselage so that trailing edges align.

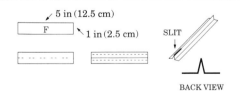

5 in (12.5 cm)

F

1 in (2.5 cm)

SLIT

BACK VIEW

STEP 18 Measure and cut a piece of paper F to dimensions shown. Mountain fold in half horizontally. Unfold. Then valley fold so that the outer edges meet center crease. Unfold. At one end, cut 1 in (2.5 cm) slit along center crease. Shape folds as shown.

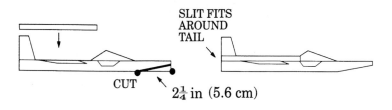

SLIT FITS
AROUND
TAIL

CUT

$2\frac{1}{4}$ in (5.6 cm)

STEP 19 Measure and cut nose diagonally along heavy line, as shown. Glue F onto top of fuselage, as shown, aligning at trailing edge.

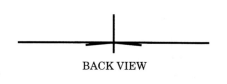

BACK VIEW

STEP 20 Adjust wings to be level.

DH108 Swallow

BACKGROUND INFORMATION

Beyond a certain speed conventional airplanes become less controllable and propellers lose their efficiency. When aircraft approach the speed of sound (about 760 mph) their control becomes unpredictable due to air resistance. For high speed flight a new shape of airplane was needed. For propulsion, designers turned to rockets and jets, which don't need propellers. In the quest for greater speed, Messerschmitt experimented with a rocket propelled airplane during the war, the ME163. After the war, deHavilland used the information gained to build the similar, but jet engined, experimental DH108 Swallow. It had wings that swept back and no horizontal stabilizers. In 1946 it flew over 600 mph. This paper airplane is modeled on the deHavilland Swallow.

TECHNICAL INFORMATION

Sweepback: Every increase in speed increases drag. Below a speed of about 250 mph air molecules easily move around a well streamlined airplane's surfaces. As speed is increased, however, the molecules cannot move out of the way quickly enough and their resistance piles them up into a pressure ridge ahead of the wings, something like a snowplow pushing snow. This build-up of pressure (drag) makes it difficult to fly the airplane, and at the speed of sound it can become dangerous. Sweeping the wings back away from the fuselage and making them broader delayed the pressure build-up until a greater speed was reached. This resulted in wings that maintain their efficiency, safely allowing planes to fly faster.

The experimental Swallow was built to test high speed flight. But even with swept-back wings, when this plane reached the speed of sound, the pressure build-up was great enough to break the airplane, and it crashed.

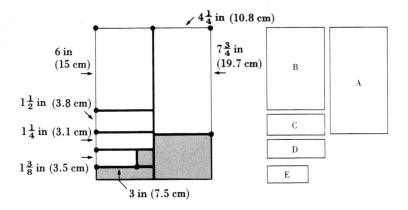

STEP 1 Measure and cut the various pieces, as shown.

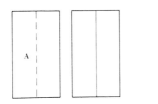

STEP 2 Lay piece A flat in a vertical direction. To make the fuselage, fold in half vertically using a valley fold. Unfold.

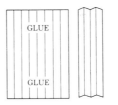

STEP 3 Valley fold each outer edge to meet center crease, as shown.

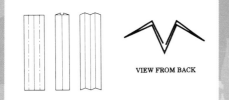

VIEW FROM BACK

GLUE

GLUE

STEP 4 Fold each side again using a mountain fold, so that outer edges meet center crease at back. Then adjust folds so that paper looks like an upside-down W, as shown.

STEP 5 Unfold fuselage completely. Refold applying glue to all contacting surfaces, as shown. Make sure fuselage is straight.

$2\frac{1}{2}$ in
(6.3 cm)

A

B

STEP 6 On each side, measure from top (front of fuselage) and mountain fold along broken lines, as shown in enlarged view A. Then flip over fuselage. On each side, valley fold triangle along broken lines, matching fold line to existing crease, as shown in enlarged view B.

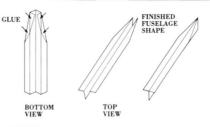

STEP 7 Glue triangles. Hold in place until glue sets. It is important that the fuselage stays straight. Do not glue nose yet.

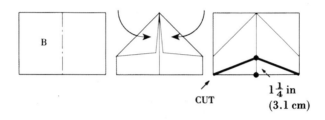

STEP 8 Use piece B to make the wings. Lay paper flat in a horizontal direction. Mountain fold in half vertically. Unfold. Then fold each side diagonally so that upper edges meet center crease. Unfold. Measure and cut trailing (back) edge, as shown by heavy line.

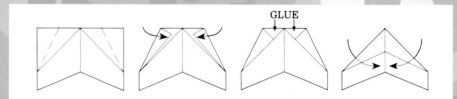

STEP 9 On each side, valley fold diagonally so that outer edge meets previously made diagonal crease. Then apply glue to upper tip only and refold along original diagonal creases.

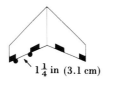

$1\frac{1}{4}$ in (3.1 cm)

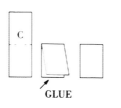

C

GLUE

STEP 10 Flip wings over. On each side, make ailerons and elevators in locations shown (see page 14).

> **AILERONS** $\frac{1}{2}$ in x $\frac{1}{4}$ in
> **(1.3 cm x .6 cm)**
> **ELEVATORS** $\frac{3}{4}$ in x $\frac{1}{4}$ in
> **(1.9 cm x .6 cm)**

STEP 11 Use piece C to make the vertical tail. Lay paper flat in a vertical direction. Mountain fold in half horizontally. Glue halves together.

$\frac{3}{4}$ in (1.9 cm)

$\frac{1}{2}$ in (1.3 cm)

STEP 12 Measure and cut, as shown. Make rudder in locations shown.

RUDDER $\frac{3}{4}$ in x $\frac{1}{4}$ in (1.9 cm x .6 cm)

D

SLIT
$\frac{1}{2}$ in
(1.3 cm)

BACK VIEW

STEP 13 Use piece D to make the fuselage top. Mountain fold in half horizontally. Unfold. Then valley fold so that the outer edges meet center crease. Unfold. At one end, cut slit along center crease, as indicated by heavy line. Shape folds as shown.

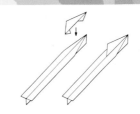

STEP 14 Use piece E to make the type 2 canopy. (See page 11.)

CANOPY (type 2) 1⅜ in x 3 in (3.5 cm x 7.5 cm) top point 2 in (5 cm)

STEP 15 Apply glue to inside of fuselage at the nose end and insert tabs on the bottom of canopy, aligning at the front. Hold until glue sets.

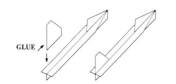

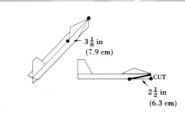

STEP 16 Apply glue to bottom part of vertical tail and insert into back of fuselage, aligning at the back edge.

STEP 17 Measure from front of fuselage and mark where to position wings. Measure and cut nose, as shown by heavy line.

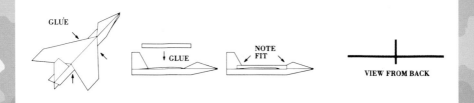

STEP 18 Glue wings to fuselage. Then glue top of fuselage in place so that slit fits around tail and front fits snuggly over back of canopy.

Mirage 2000

BACKGROUND INFORMATION

High-speed flight became common after World War II, and wings that swept back came into widespread use because of their efficiency at high speed. Filling in the space between the wingtips of swept-back wings resulted in the formation of triangle shaped wings (delta wings). Delta wings are very stable in flight and are good for supersonic flight. One of their first successful applications was in the early 1950s on the experimental Fairey Delta that exceeded 1,000 mph. Two other supersonic planes of the 1950s were the General Dynamics F106 Delta Dart and the Dassault-Breguet Mirage 3. The Mirage has been upgraded several times and is still being built as the Mirage 2000. This paper airplane is modeled on it.

TECHNICAL INFORMATION

Delta Wings: The triangle shape of these wings has a unique affect on the air flowing over their upper surfaces. The air flows diagonally towards the fuselage. Like swept-back wings, delta wings prevent the buildup of the pressure ridge created by high speed flight. In addition, the shape lends added stability, and most delta wing airplanes need no additional horizontal stabilizers. However, because they are so stable, some fighter planes have surfaces added to make them less stable and more maneuverable. Delta wings can operate at much greater angles of attack before the air flowing over the top surfaces becomes turbulent and the wings stall.

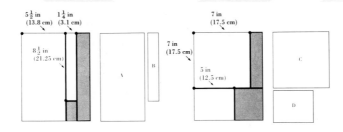

STEP 1 Measure and cut the various pieces from two sheets of bond paper.

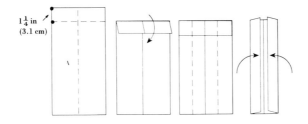

STEP 2 Lay piece A vertically to make the fuselage. Fold in half vertically using a valley fold. Unfold. Measure from top and valley fold, as shown. Valley fold each side so that outer edges meet center crease, as shown.

STEP 3 Fold each side again using a mountain fold, so that outer edges meet center crease at back. Then adjust folds so that paper looks like an upside-down W, as shown.

STEP 4 Unfold fuselage completely. Refold, applying glue to contacting surfaces, as shown. Make sure fuselage is straight.

STEP 5 On each side, measure from top (front of fuselage), mark, and mountain fold along broken lines, as shown in enlarged view A. Then flip over fuselage. On each side, valley fold triangle along broken lines, matching fold line to existing crease, as shown in enlarged view B.

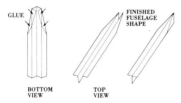

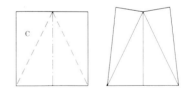

STEP 6 Glue triangles. Hold in place until glue sets. It is important that the fuselage stays straight. Do not glue nose yet.

STEP 7 Use piece C to make the wings. Mountain fold in half vertically. Unfold. Draw a line from the top center to the lower corners and valley fold along lines, as shown. Unfold.

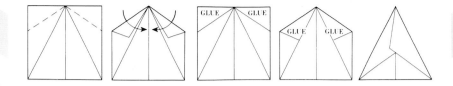

STEP 8 On each side, valley fold so that top edge meets the diagonal crease.

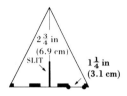

STEP 9 Unfold completely. Refold, applying glue to both sides of small upper triangles only. Flip over and finish wings. Add ailerons and elevators, in locations shown. Make slit, as shown by heavy line.

AILERONS ½ in x ¼ in (1.3 cm x .6 cm)
ELEVATORS 1 in x ¼ in (2.5 cm x .6 cm)

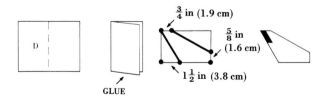

STEP 10 Lay piece D horizontally to make the vertical tail. Valley fold in half vertically. Glue halves together. Turn, as shown, measure, mark, and cut along heavy lines. Make rudder on trailing edge, as shown.

RUDDER 1 in x ¼ in (2.5 cm x .6 cm)

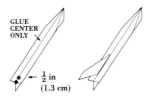

STEP 11 Apply glue to inside center only of fuselage. Measure from back of fuselage and mark, as shown. Then apply glue and slide tail into fuselage, aligning at mark.

STEP 12 Apply glue and attach wings to fuselage, slipping around vertical tail. Align trailing edge at the mark.

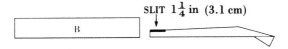

STEP 13 Use piece B to make a type 1 canopy (see page 11). Make a slit at center back of canopy.

CANOPY (type 1) 1 ¼ in x 8 ½ in (3.1 cm x 21.7 cm) top point 3 in (7.5 cm) back ⅜ in (1cm)

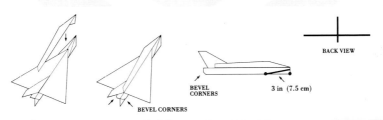

STEP 14 Apply glue to inside back of canopy and front tab of canopy. Insert tab into fuselage. The vertical tail fits into slit. Align at nose. Measure and cut front of fuselage along heavy diagonal line, as shown. To finish, bevel all corners on fuselage back, as shown.

Glider

BACKGROUND INFORMATION

While Wilber Wright was mainly interested in powered flight, his brother Orville experimented with gliders. Both types of flight continued to be developed. By the time World War II ended much had been learned about good aerodynamic performance. During the 1950s and 60s the design of gliders was greatly improved as builders produced low-drag gliders with highly efficient wings. With long soaring flight now possible, Orville's dream of sustained motorless flight was fulfilled. In Europe, Germany became well known for its gliders. In the USA, the Schweizer brothers of New York built good training gliders that did much to promote gliding in North America. Soaring became a popular sport the world over. This paper airplane is modeled on gliders.

TECHNICAL INFORMATION

Aspect Ratio: Wings that are short have a low aspect ratio. Wings that are long and slender have a high aspect ratio. Wings with a high aspect ratio produce more lift for the amount of drag they create. This makes them suitable for gliders, where the smallest amount of drag possible is best. Today's gliders are very efficient. They soar like the eagles. From an altitude of 6,000 ft (1,800 m) some of them can fly about 60 nautical miles forward without any additional lift. To gain altitude, pilots usually take advantage of columns of rising air. (This is air that has been warmed by the ground on a sunny day, making it lighter and consequently making is rise.) Some glider pilots have remained airborne for more than ten hours and flown distances of more than 1,000 nautical miles without landing. They have reached altitudes of more than 40,000 ft (12,000 m). Because the columns of rising air are invisible, it takes skill, and sometimes luck, to find and stay in them. Many countries have national gliding competitions where the best pilots demonstrate their skills.

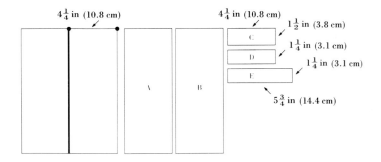

STEP 1 Measure and cut a piece of bond paper, as shown. Three additional pieces are needed, as shown.

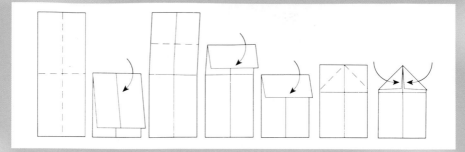

STEP 2 To make the fuselage, fold piece A in half vertically using a valley fold. Unfold. Valley fold in half horizontally. Unfold. Then valley fold so that upper edge meets horizontal crease. Refold original horizontal crease. Then on each side, valley fold diagonally so that top edge meets center crease.

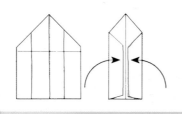

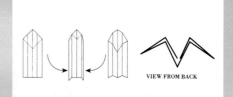

STEP 3 Valley fold each side so that outer edges meet center crease, as shown.

STEP 4 Fold again using a mountain fold, so that outer edges meet center crease at back. Then adjust folds so that paper looks like an upside-down W, as shown.

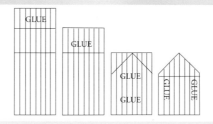

STEP 5 Unfold fuselage completely. Refold, applying glue to contacting surfaces, as shown. Make sure fuselage is straight.

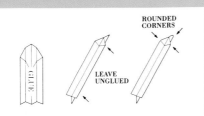

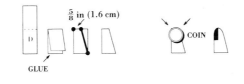

STEP 6 Glue center of fuselage, leaving 1 in (2.5 cm) at the nose and 1 in (2.5 cm) at the tail end unglued. Round corners at nose end.

STEP 7 On each side, measure and cut fuselage back, as shown by heavy lines.

STEP 8 Lay piece D vertically to make the vertical tail. Valley fold in half horizontally. Glue halves together. Measure and cut leading edge along heavy line, as shown. Trace around a ³/₄ in (1.9 cm) coin and cut out to round corners. On trailing edge, make rudder.

RUDDER ³/₄ in x ¹/₄ in (1.9 cm x .6 cm)

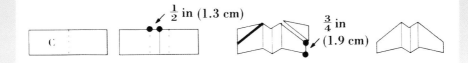

STEP 9 Use piece C to make the horizontal tail. Valley fold in half vertically. Unfold. On each side, measure from center crease, as shown, and mountain fold. On each side, measure and cut leading edges along heavy lines, as shown.

Glider | 61

STEP 10 Trace around a coin and cut out to make all the corners rounded. On trailing edges, make elevators (see page 14).

ELEVATOR 1¼ in x ¼ in (3.1 cm x .6 cm)

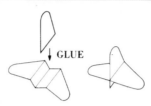

STEP 11 Apply glue to inside of horizontal tail and insert vertical tail, aligning trailing edges.

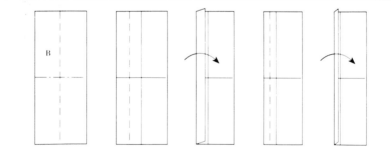

STEP 12 Use piece B to make the wings. Fold in half horizontally, using a mountain fold. Unfold. Fold in half vertically, using a valley fold. Unfold. Then valley fold so that outer edge meets center crease. Fold same side again so that outer edge again meets center crease. Refold original horizontal center crease.

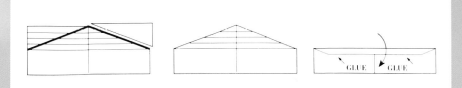

STEP 13 Unfold completely. On each side, draw and cut diagonally along heavy lines, as shown. Refold. Apply glue before refolding original horizontal center crease only. The folded over part is the bottom of the leading edge (front) of the wings. These slender wings are quite fragile. When they are completed, make sure they are not twisted.

STEP 14 Measure and cut trailing edge (back) of wings, as shown by heavy lines. Then trace around a coin and cut out to make rounded corners at both leading edges and trailing edges, as shown.

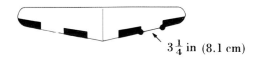

STEP 15 At wingtips on trailing edges, make ailerons. Then make secondary control surfaces (flaps), in locations shown.

AILERONS ³/₄ in x ¹/₄ in (1.9 cm x .6 cm)
FLAPS 1 ¹/₄ in x ¹/₄ in (3.1 cm x .6 cm)

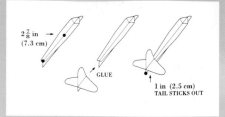 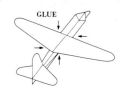

STEP 16 Measure from back of fuselage and mark position of leading edge (front) of wing. Apply glue and slide tail into back of fuselage.

STEP 17 At the mark, attach wings to fuselage.

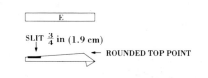

STEP 18 Make a type 1 canopy, using piece E (see page 11). Make a slit at the center back, as shown. Round the top point slightly.

CANOPY (type 1) 1 ¼ in x 5 ¾ in (3.1 cm x 14.6 cm) top point 1 in (2.5 cm) back ¼ in (.6 cm)

STEP 19 Apply glue to inside back and front tab of canopy. Insert tab into fuselage, sliding vertical tail into slit. Align at nose.

STEP 20 Measure and cut back of fuselage along heavy diagonal line, as shown. Adjust dihedral (upward slanting of wings and tail), as shown.

FSW Concept

BACKGROUND INFORMATION

Airplane builders are always trying to make planes that are more suited to special tasks. In the 1980s a new shape of airplane appeared. Grumman introduced the X29 forward swept wing (FSW) experimental airplane, using new composite materials that were very light and strong. Such a design was impossible to build with traditional materials. The advantages of sweeping the wings forward instead of backward allow for maneuverability and high angle of attack flight—desirable qualities for military application. This paper airplane is modeled on a forward swept wing aircraft that has not yet been built. This concept, designed by Grumman, is being considered for possible future development.

TECHNICAL INFORMATION

A future fighter will have to operate over a wide range of speeds, be very maneuverable, and be fuel efficient. It will have to be able to land in very small spaces. Forward swept wings combined with strakes (extensions of the leading edges near the fuselage) will improve the flight characteristics of the plane at very low and very high speeds. However, having no horizontal tail makes the plane sensitive to correct balance, and computers will aid in control. The light weight of composites, the lack of a horizontal tail, and better engines will allow improved fuel efficiency. The FSW Concept will probably have two turbojet engines and be able to fly at more than twice the speed of sound at high altitudes. Its air intakes will be part of the large strakes. The plane will have a missile rail at each wingtip, and be able to carry extra fuel tanks and a variety of armament under the wings. Like present day fighters, this craft will be used for both air-to-air and air-to-ground operations. Besides its military role, this airplane could be a good candidate for aerial display at air shows.

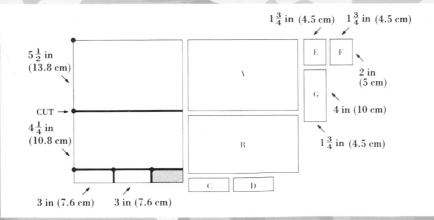

STEP 1 Measure and cut pieces from a sheet of bond paper. Three additional pieces, E, F, and G are needed, as shown.

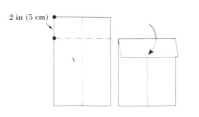

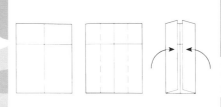

STEP 2 To make the fuselage, lay piece A in a vertical direction. Fold in half vertically, using a valley fold. Unfold. Measure from top and valley fold, as shown.

STEP 3 Valley fold so that outer edges meet center crease, as shown.

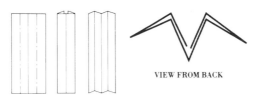

VIEW FROM BACK

STEP 4 Fold again using a mountain fold, so that outer edges meet center crease at back. Then adjust folds so that paper looks like an upside-down W, as shown.

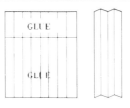

GLUE

GLUE

STEP 5 Unfold fuselage completely. Refold, applying glue to contacting surfaces, as shown. Make sure fuselage is straight.

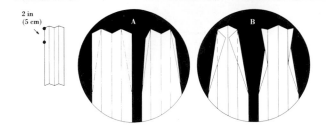

STEP 6 On each side, measure from top (front of fuselage), mark, and mountain fold along broken lines, as shown in enlarged view A. Then flip over fuselage. On each side, valley fold triangle along broken lines, matching fold line to existing crease, as shown in enlarged view B.

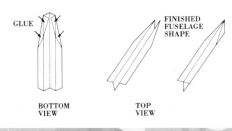

STEP 7 Glue triangles. Hold in place until glue sets. It is important that the fuselage stays straight. Do not glue nose yet.

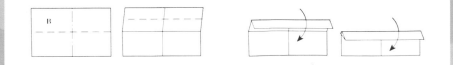

STEP 8 Use piece B to make the wings. Lay paper in a horizontal direction and fold in half vertically, using a mountain fold. Unfold. Valley fold in half horizontally. Unfold. Then valley fold horizontally so that top edge meets center crease. Fold over again along original center crease.

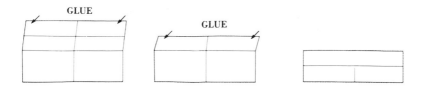

STEP 9 Unfold completely. Refold, applying glue to no more than 1 in (2.5 cm) from outer tips, as shown. The folded over part is the bottom of the leading edge (front) of the wings.

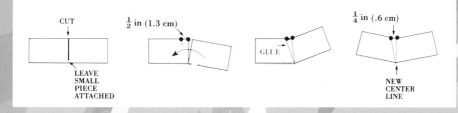

STEP 10 To sweep wings forward, cut along center line from the leading edge, leaving a small piece attached at the trailing edge (back). Then measure and make a mark on leading edge, as shown. Align pieces to the mark. Glue. Measure and draw new center line.

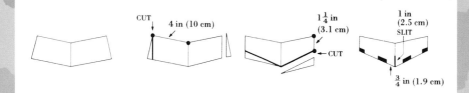

STEP 11 To finish forward swept wings, measure and cut wing tips along heavy lines. Then cut trailing edge along heavy lines, as shown. On trailing edges (back), make ailerons and elevators (see page 14). From trailing edge, make a slit along center line, as shown.

AILERONS ½ in x ¼ in (1.3 cm x .6 cm)
ELEVATORS 1 in x ³/₈ in (2.5 cm x 1 cm)

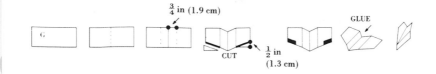

STEP 12 Use piece G to make the twin vertical tails. Lay paper in a horizontal direction. Valley fold in half vertically. Unfold. On each side, measure from center crease and mountain fold, as shown. Then measure and cut trailing edges, as shown by heavy lines. Make rudders. Glue center.

RUDDERS 1 in x ³/₈ in (2.5 cm x 1 cm)

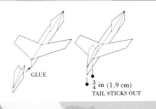

STEP 13 Use piece C to make a type 2 canopy (see page 11).

CANOPY (type 2) 1 ¼ in X 3 in (3.1 cm X 7.5 cm) top point 1 ³/₄ in (4.5 cm)

STEP 14 Apply glue to inside of nose and the small triangular tabs on the bottom of canopy. Slide tabs into fuselage, aligning canopy with the tip of the nose. Hold until glue sets.

STEP 15 Glue wings in place, aligning at the trailing (back) edge. Make sure they are centered and at right angles to the fuselage. Trim fuselage back flush with the wing trailing (back) edges.

STEP 16 Measure and mark along bottom of tail. Apply glue and slide tail into back of fuselage (and slit in the wings) to the mark.

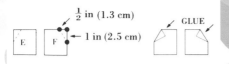

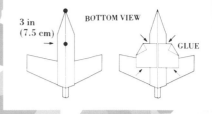

STEP 17 Use pieces E and F to make the strakes. Lay pieces vertically side by side, as shown. Measure on outer left and right edges and valley fold diagonally, as shown. Glue.

STEP 18 Turn airplane over. Measure from front and mark as shown. On each side, glue strakes in place, aligning inside corners to the mark.

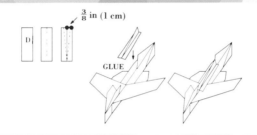

STEP 19 Lay piece D in a vertical direction to make the fuselage top. Mountain fold in half vertically. Unfold. On each side, measure and valley fold. Adjust shape, as shown. Glue onto top of fuselage, as shown, fitting the front snugly over back of canopy.

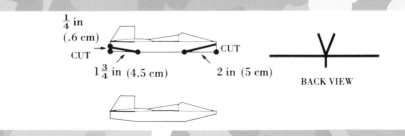

STEP 20 Measure and cut nose and tail diagonally, as shown by heavy lines. This plane has no dihedral. Twin tails are canted (tilted), as shown.

SST Concept

BACKGROUND INFORMATION

Flying faster than the speed of sound can only be done in areas of the world where no people live, because the loud sonic boom would break the windows in people's houses. Therefore, supersonic flights are undertaken only between cities across the world's oceans. However, the Sukoi and Gulfstream airplane companies are experimenting with planes of different shapes and sizes to see if they can reduce the intensity of the sonic boom. If the boom can be made quieter, supersonic air service between cities on the same continent or even in the same country would be possible. This paper airplane is modeled on a plane that has not yet been built. It is a concept of a future supersonic transport plane (SST).

TECHNICAL INFORMATION

The type of airplane being planned is probably small, carrying no more than ten passengers. This small size would be one way of making the boom produced in supersonic flight less damaging. The goal is to make the plane capable of traveling nearly twice the speed of sound. It will probably be built of lightweight composite materials and use computers for flight control. The plane's main wings will be delta wings with winglets at the tips. Winglets help direct the airflow over the wings. Canard wings for added control will also be used. This plane might be the business jet of the future.

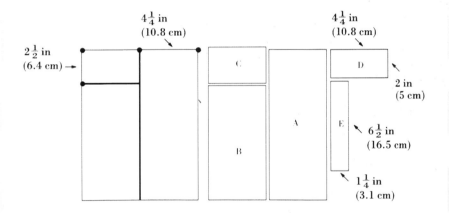

STEP 1 Measure and cut the various pieces from a sheet of bond paper. Two additional pieces, D and E, are needed, as shown.

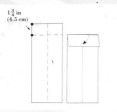

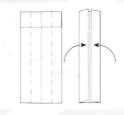

STEP 2 To make the fuselage, fold piece A in half vertically using a valley fold. Unfold. Measure from top and valley fold, as shown.

STEP 3 Valley fold each side so that outer edges meet center crease, as shown.

VIEW FROM BACK

STEP 4 Fold each side again using a mountain fold, so that outer edges meet center crease at back. Then adjust folds so that paper looks like an upside-down W, as shown.

STEP 5 Unfold fuselage completely. Refold applying glue to contacting surfaces, as shown. Make sure fuselage is straight.

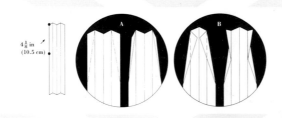

STEP 6 On each side, measure from top (front of fuselage), mark, and mountain fold along broken lines, as shown in enlarged view A. Then flip over fuselage. On each side, valley fold triangle along broken lines, matching fold line to existing crease, as shown in enlarged view B.

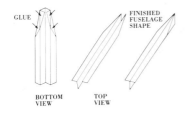 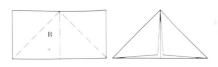

STEP 7 Glue triangles. Hold in place until glue sets. It is important that the fuselage stays straight. Do not glue nose yet.

STEP 8 Lay piece B flat in a horizontal direction to make the wings. Fold in half vertically, using a mountain fold. Unfold. On each side, valley fold diagonally so that top edge meets center crease, as shown.

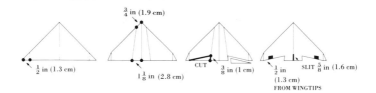

STEP 9 Unfold diagonal folds. On each side, valley fold diagonally so that outer edges meet diagonal crease, as shown. Apply glue to small upper triangles only and refold original diagonal creases.

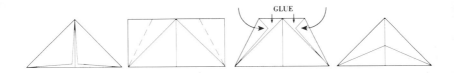

STEP 10 Flip wings over. To make winglets, measure at each wingtip and valley fold, as shown. Then on each side, measure and draw lines, as shown. At the trailing edge, measure and cut, as shown by heavy lines. Make ailerons in locations shown. Measure and cut a slit in location shown.

AILERONS ½ in × ¼ in (1.3 cm × .6 cm)

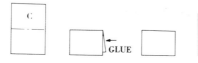

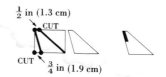

STEP 11 Lay piece C in a vertical direction. Mountain fold in half horizontally to make the vertical tail. Glue halves together.

STEP 12 Measure and draw lines, as shown. Cut diagonally, as shown by heavy lines. Make the rudder, as shown.

RUDDERS 1 in x ¼ in (2.5 cm x .6 cm)

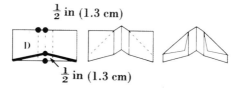

STEP 13 Lay piece D in a horizontal direction to make canard wings. Mountain fold in half vertically. Unfold. Measure from bottom along center crease and cut, as shown by heavy lines. On each side, measure and valley fold. Then on each side, fold diagonally so that top edge meets vertical crease.

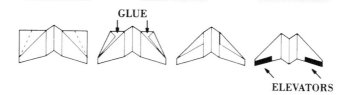

STEP 14 Unfold diagonal folds. On each side, valley fold diagonally so that outer edges meet diagonal creases, as shown. Apply glue to small upper triangles only and refold original diagonal creases. Flip wings over and make elevators in locations shown.

ELEVATORS 1⅛ in x ¼ in (2.8 cm x .6 cm)

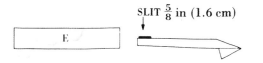

SLIT $\frac{5}{8}$ in (1.6 cm)

E

STEP 15 Use piece E to make a type 1 canopy (see page 11).

**CANOPY (type 1) 1 ¼ in x 6 ½ in (3.1 cm x 16.5 cm)
top point 1 ¾ in (4.5 cm) back ⅜ in (1 cm)**

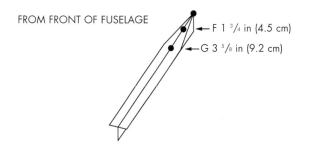

FROM FRONT OF FUSELAGE

F 1 ¾ in (4.5 cm)

G 3 ⅝ in (9.2 cm)

STEP 16 Measure from front of fuselage and make marks for positioning the leading edges of canard wings and canopy at F and main wings at G, as shown.

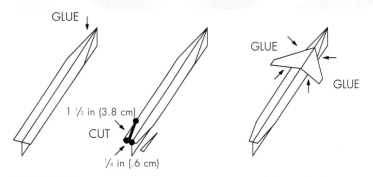

GLUE

GLUE

GLUE

1 ½ in (3.8 cm)

CUT

¼ in (.6 cm)

STEP 17 Apply glue to inside of nose, no more than 1 in (2.5 cm) from tip. Hold until glue sets. Then measure and cut back of fuselage, as shown. Glue canard wings in place. (Do not glue the inside center of the canard wings.)

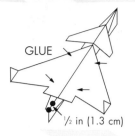

GLUE

½ in (1.3 cm)

STEP 18 Glue main wings in place, making sure they are centered and at right angles to the fuselage. Then measure from back of fuselage and mark.

STEP 19 Apply glue and slide vertical tail into back of fuselage so that trailing edge aligns with mark.

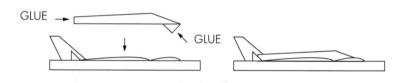

GLUE →

GLUE

STEP 20 Apply glue to the tabs on the bottom of canopy and the inside back of the canopy. Slide tab into center of canard wings with the slit fitting around the vertical tail. Align canopy front with front of canard wings.

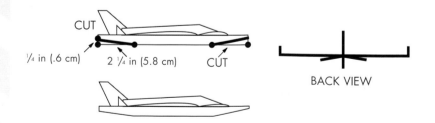

CUT

¼ in (.6 cm)   2 ¼ in (5.8 cm)   CUT

BACK VIEW

STEP 21 Measure and cut nose and tail, as shown by heavy lines. The wings of this airplane have no dihedral. Adjust winglets to a vertical position.

Glossary

ANGLE OF ATTACK The downward slant, from front to back, of a wing.

ANGLE OF BANK The raising of the outside wing and lowering of the inside wing during a turn.

ASPECT RATIO The length of a wing in relation to its width. The longer a wing, the higher its aspect ratio.

ATTITUDE The direction an airplane is pointing in relation to the horizon (banking, yawing, or pitching).

BALLAST Extra weight needed in the nose of an airplane to make the center of gravity coincide with the wings, which provide the lift.

CONTROL SURFACES Small surfaces that can be bent to alter the airflow and change an airplane's attitude—ailerons for bank, elevators for pitch, and rudders for yaw.

DIHEDRAL ANGLE Upward slanting of wings away from the fuselage. (Downward slanting is called anhedral.)

DRAG The resistance of air on moving objects, slowing them down.

FUSELAGE The body of an airplane.

LEADING EDGES The front edges of wings, tails, or other parts.

LIFT The force of air pressure beneath the wings buoying up an airplane.

MANEUVER Skillfully making an airplane fly in a desired direction—turn, climb, dive, stall, spin, or loop.

PITCH Nose-up or nose-down attitude.

ROLL Rotation along the length of an airplane.

SPAR The main internal frame that supports the wing.

STRAKES Wedge-shaped extensions of the wing's leading (front) edges near the fuselage.

TRAILING EDGES The back edges of wings, tails, or other parts.

TRIM Making small adjustments to the control surfaces to affect the attitude of an airplane.

TRIM DRAG The drag (resistance) produced from bending control surfaces into the airflow.

VENTRAL FIN A small stabilizer on each side of the fuselage underneath the tail.

WING LOADING The amount of weight a given area of wing is required to lift.

YAW Nose-left or nose-right attitude.

Index